Ask BIG

Terri Savelle Foy

978-1-942126-24-9

Terri Savelle Foy Ministries
Post Office Box 1959
Rockwall, TX 75087

www.terri.com

Printed in the United States of America
First Edition 2021

Contents

Introduction

My goal of this book is to help you build your faith. Romans 10:17 (NKJV) says, "Faith comes by hearing, and hearing by the word of God." So every time you hear the Word of God through listening to or reading motivational, faith-building messages, your faith gets stronger.

I like to think of building your faith like brushing teeth. You could say, "I have brushed my teeth 50,000 times now. Can I stop?" Well you could, but it would be gross. And eventually decay will set in. It won't be overnight. It will be a process of decay. It's the same way with your faith. You could say, "Terri, I have listened to 12,000 faith-building messages and read 145 faith-building books. Can I stop?" Well you could, but little by little, your faith is going to get smaller. Because the Bible says, faith comes by hearing. What that also means is that faith goes by *not* hearing.

When you were born again, you were given the measure of faith (Romans 12:3). Every single one of us were given the exact same measure, just like when we were born, every one of us were given the exact same muscles. So what's the difference in a body-builder's muscles and a 12-year-old's muscles? The difference is a body-builder has developed their muscles to a greater degree so they can handle more weight.

Do you know it's the same with faith? You see some people who are believing for millions of dollars and others who are believing to put gas in their car. What's the difference? The person believing for millions of dollars has just built their faith to a greater degree, so they can believe for more.

I believe my faith muscles are like a spiritual body-builder, and that's what I want you to feel like on the inside when you finish reading this little book. I want your faith so strong in what God's about to do in your life that there's no force from hell that can stop you from living your dreams.

Let me give you one more example to illustrate this. Having faith for what may look like an impossible dream is like taking a pill. When a doctor prescribes a pill, you swallow it, then the pill goes down your throat, to your stomach, and makes your headache go away. I do not understand how that works, but if I do what the doctor says, I'm going to get the results he says I can get, right? God's Word is the same way. I do not understand how having faith in my heart can make the dreams on my vision board come to pass. But if I do what God says to do, I can have the results that He says I can have. I know, it's a big pill to swallow. (Do you see what I did there?) But we're going to take God at His Word.

I'm believing that as you read the following pages your faith is going to be built like never before to go after your dreams.

CHAPTER 1

Ask

Since the 1970s my dad, Jerry Savelle, has done mission work in Africa. His ministry has built orphanages and medical clinics, trained pastors, built water wells for widows, and done so much. In those early days, Oral Roberts heard that my dad was doing all of this work in Africa. So he asked my dad if he could go on one of his trips and see first-hand what he was doing and get involved in it. Floored and honored, my dad agreed, of course. He was so excited (to say the least) because Oral Roberts was one of his heroes. They flew to Africa together.

Their first big meeting was to open a medical clinic in Kenya. The President of Kenya was there, as well as other heads of state and several medical doctors. As the President of Kenya stood at the podium speaking, my dad, Oral Roberts, and all of these other government dignitaries sat on stage behind the podium.

As they were listening to the President of Kenya, Oral Roberts grabbed a napkin off the table and started writing something. After a moment, he handed the napkin to my dad and he said, "Read this."

Dad couldn't understand what the napkin said, so he leaned over discreetly and whispered to Oral Roberts, "I can't read this."

Oral Roberts said, "Read it again."

Dad looked at it, but still couldn't read it. Oral Roberts told him to try again. By then, people were watching them. So my dad looked at the napkin, and this is what it said: Strebor Laro. Dad sighed and told him, "I don't understand what this means."

In front of all of the people watching, he leaned over to my dad and said, "That's Oral Roberts spelled backwards."

"What?" Taken aback, my dad said, "Why are you writing Oral Roberts backwards?"

Do you know what Oral Roberts said? "Because I'm bored." He said, "I'm bored by their small thinking." And then he said, "I'm bored by your small plans."

So here's my question for you. Is God bored? Is He sitting up in heaven scribbling DOG (God backwards)? Is He bored like a dog because of your small thinking?

Up Your Ask

I was out walking one morning when I heard the Lord say to me, "Ask me for something big." That phrase kept playing over and over in my head as I walked. When I got home, I pulled my journal out and I heard the Lord say, "Ask big and believe it's done." Then He continued, "If it's in your heart, it's there for a reason."

I believe the Bible is the number one success book ever written. Everything we need to achieve our dreams and fulfill our purpose can be found in this success book. And the Author of this success book says in Matthew 7:7–8, "Ask and it will be given to you. Seek, and you will find; knock, and it will opened to you. For everyone who asks receives, and the one who seeks finds, and to the one who knocks it will be opened. How much more will your Father who is in heaven give good things to those who ask him!" Those verses are not just in some people's Bible. It's in every Bible. It's in *your* Bible.

I did a little research and found there are 100 scriptures in the Bible where God tells us to request or ask for things. When God says something once, He means it. When God says something 100 times, you better believe He's trying to get your attention.

Could we seriously be missing out on some things because we aren't asking God?

Just One Question

So let's break down the statement the Lord shared with me, "Ask big and believe it's done." The first word He said is "Ask."

Steve Harvey tells the story about his mother ingraining seven words in his mind: You have not because you ask not. He said,

"Most of you are not living your dreams because you're not asking for the life of your dreams." He continued, "If you will up your ask, God will up His give." Now I love that phrase. Is it really that simple? John 16:24 says, "Until now, you have asked for nothing in My name; ask and you will receive, that your joy may be full."

Businesses have caught on to this principle. Years ago, McDonald's trained their staff to ask one more question when somebody ordered a hamburger and a drink. Do you know what that question was? "Would you like fries with that?" Apparently, a lot of people said, "Sure, why not?" because that single question raised their bottom line more than $20 million the first year they implemented this question. You have not because you ask not.

In fundraising, the number one reason donations are not received is because the organizations don't ask. In fact, I've been to some of the most dazzling fundraisers that were so elegant they had my jaw dropping, but at the end of the night, there was no ask for donations or the ask was vague and unclear. So they didn't receive any. And the event left the nonprofit in a financial hole. Ask and you shall receive.

Have you noticed at some of the grocery stores when you check out they'll ask you, "Would you like to round up to the nearest dollar and give the difference to a charity?" A research team decided to partner with a nonprofit zoo to experiment with that question. When their patrons were ordering food, they asked, "Would you like to round up to the nearest dollar?" In response, 45% of the people they asked said, "Sure!" They raised 21% more money just by asking, "Would you like to round up?"

Our ministry YouTube channel is another great example of this principle. I had the YouTube channel going for years and we had almost no subscribers. Do you know why? I never asked for any. All of a sudden, it dawned on me, I'm supposed to ask viewers to subscribe. When I started opening or closing the weekly video by saying, "Would you take a moment and push that little red arrow? It lets me and YouTube know that you want Christian motivation," people started pushing the arrow. Now we're well over 200,000 subscribers.

Asking is a biblical principle that the world has discovered works. God means what He says when He says, "You have not because you ask not."

Asking is a clear key to success in business, in ministry, and in life.

Ask Your Way to Success

There was a young woman, Wendy Stehling, who hated her working environment at an advertising agency so she wanted to start her own agency but didn't have the money to get it going. She knew she needed $100,000. So she began asking people, "What is the quickest way to raise $100,000?" The most popular answer she got was to sell a book. She did the math and decided to write a book that could sell 100,000 copies in 90 days for $1 each. If she could do that, she could raise the money she needed to start her own agency.

Stehling didn't know what kind of book to write. So she started asking what kind of book 100,000 people would want to buy. After discovering the best-selling books in America were weight loss books, she asked herself, "How do I distinguish myself as an expert in the field?" Guess what she decided to do? Ask other women! She gathered focus groups and asked, "If you could only lose weight in one part of your body, which part would you choose?" Overwhelmingly women said, "My thighs."

Then she followed up with, "When would you want to lose it?" And most of them said, "In April or May in time for swimsuit season." All she did was what they told her to do. She wrote a book called, *Thin Thighs in 30 Days* and released it in April. By June, she had her $100,000. When asked how she reached her goal, her answer was, "I asked my way to success."

God's the One who said,

If you lack wisdom, ask me for it.
I'll give it to you generously.

James 1:5

So often we ask one thing one time and if what we are looking for doesn't happen, we quit. If Wendy Stehling had only asked the first question, she may not have had such success, but she kept asking and followed up with more asking.

Take a look at these sales statistics:

- 44% of salespeople quit after the first call.
- 24% quit after the second call.
- 14% quit after the third call.
- 12% quit after the fourth call.

If you add these numbers up, 94% of all salespeople quit after the fourth call. But are you ready for this: 60% of sales are made after the fourth call.

Ask, ask, and keep on asking.

Gandhi said it another way, "If you don't ask, you don't get." That's deep, isn't it?

There's a reason God repeats Himself 100 times in the Bible. He wants us to ask Him for the dreams in our heart. I have a vivid memory of sitting on a little bench in Paris, France by the Eiffel Tower. I was reminded of the verse, "Ask of Me, and I will give you the nations" (Psalm 2:8). I sat there in Paris and said, "Lord,

I'm asking You for France. I'm asking You for an opportunity to make an impact in this nation." Right after that God started opening up doors of opportunity for me in that nation. (Later I'll mention another important step I took that made this possible.) So you can see throughout the Word, He says to ask.

What Are You Asking For?

Tony Robbins often tells the story of when he first started learning about success. He had such a poverty mentality that his mentor, Jim Rohn, began to teach him how to change his outlook on life. So Jim Rohn had Tony get $300 out of his bank. He wasn't to spend it, but to place the bills in his wallet in front of the rest of his cash. He did this so that the hundred dollar bills were the first things he saw every time he open his wallet. Rohn told Tony to start conditioning himself to see prosperity and wealth. Rohn made this powerful statement, "God's Word says to ask and you shall receive. Life will pay you any price you ask of it, but you've got to start asking." Obviously Tony Robbins changed his whole mindset. He became one of the top success coaches in the world.

Years later, Tony Robbins spoke at a conference in Boston. When he exited the building, a homeless man came up and asked him for money. Tony thought, *I'm going to practice this on this man.* He took a coin out of his pocket as well as the $300 out of his wallet, and he held it up to the homeless man. He repeated to the man what Rohn had taught him, "Listen, life will pay you any price you ask of it. God's Word says to come boldly to the throne and ask for what you need. Ask and you shall receive."

That homeless man looked at him, looked at the money, looked at the coin, looked back at him, looked at the money, looked at the coin, and then he said, "You're weird." But that's not all he did. The homeless man grabbed the coin and ran off. That homeless man asked for what he thought he was worth. He didn't think he was worth the $300. He only felt worthy of that single coin.

When you think about that story and your life, what are you asking God for? You will ask Him for what you think you are worth. Are you asking God to put gas in your car or to pay the car off?

God is the One who told us to come boldly to the throne and ask for what we need (Hebrews 4:6). Be crystal clear on what you're asking.

Even in market research they've discovered that the more clearly you ask, the better your results. In fact, researchers went to a bus station and asked random travelers, "Do you have any change I could borrow?" In turn, 44%

responded favorably giving them some change. For the second test, the researchers were very clear. When they said, "Can I borrow a quarter?" 64% responded. Then they clarified their ask even further. When they asked for 37 cents, 75% responded. The more precise and clear you are, the better the results.

The same is true with God. You could be saying, "Lord, I'm asking You for increase." If you are not specific on how much increase, you could be given $20 and there's your increase.

You may have heard the story I've told before about a minister named Kenneth Hagin. He would see people praying at church, gently tap them on the shoulder, and ask, "Sweetheart, what are you praying for?" So many times people would answer, "Oh, nothing in particular." Then he would say, "Then that's exactly what you're going to get. Nothing in particular." That's not what God wants for you!

God wants you to be specific for what you're believing for.

Think about it this way. At Christmastime, when you ask your children what they want, do your kids say, "Dad, I want presents. Mom, I just want some gifts." No, they make a Pinterest board and send you links to everything they want, right?

Similarly, God wants you to be specific about what you want.

Word of Our Testimony

"Are you surprised at what God has done in your life and ministry?" I get this question a lot, especially from those who knew me before or know my story of how drastically my life has changed. My answer is the same every time: I am truly overwhelmed with gratitude. I think I say "Thank You, Jesus" 75 times a day, because

I am so grateful for what God has done and I never want to take it for granted. But I'm not surprised. I'm not saying that to sound arrogant at all. The reason I'm not surprised is because every single thing that's happening in my life and through our ministry right now, I've asked God for it.

I only know how to teach something through my own experience, and Revelations 12:11 tells us to use the word of our testimony. So I want to build your faith with some of my own stories.

Years ago I had a dream in my heart to write a book and see it in bookstores. I went to a bookstore and posed in front of the bookshelves as if my book was there. Even though I hadn't written a book. Now I never want to direct you to do something that is not in the Word of God. So let's just see if what I'm saying lines up with God's Word. What does God say?

Therefore I tell you, whatever you ask for in prayer believe that you have received it, and it will be yours.

Mark 11:24

He said to ask. So was it a coincidence that a few months later I got a call from a woman who wanted to represent me as my literary agent? I didn't even know that's what they were called! She pitched my book to publishers and got me in the bookstores. Is that a coincidence? Not one bit.

God can make things happen for you that you could never make happen on your own when you start asking.

I wrote down five foreign languages into which I wanted my books translated. One of them was German. I don't know anybody in

Germany. I don't speak German. At the time, I'd never even been to Germany. But German was one of the languages that I had on my heart. Again, let's see what God's Word says. "If you ask me anything in my name, I will do it" (John 14:14). It is no coincidence that seven months after I wrote that vision down, we got an email from an organization in Germany inviting me to speak at a conference, where they told me the number one Christian publisher in Germany wanted to meet and talk with me about getting my books translated. Now we have four ministry books translated into German.

God will put you on the hearts of people in another nation when you start asking Him for big things.

This next example is not super spiritual, but I had a desire in my heart to write one of my books in an apartment in Paris. When I wrote that vision down, I couldn't afford to take two or three weeks and just go to France and write my next book. But you know what, I decided to take God at His Word, and His Word says, "If you abide in Me, and My words abide in you, ask whatever you wish, and it will be done for you" (John 15:7). Yes, it says that! Ask whatever you wish. It is no coincidence that I wrote the book *5 Things Successful People Do Before 8 AM* in a Parisian apartment with a view of the Eiffel Tower.

I set another faith goal one year that Rodney and I would pay off the eight acres of land we have to build our dream house on. I didn't just write the vision down; I also did the math. I added up all the numbers and there was no way. It was absolutely impossible that we could pay off our land that quickly. But I decided to take God at His Word where it says, "Again I say to you, if two of you agree on earth about anything they ask, it will be done for them by my Father in heaven" (Matthew 18:19).

Rodney and I make two, don't we? By September 2nd that year we paid off our land.

Last example I'll share with you is my dream is to teach teenagers how to get a vision and plan for their lives. At my Icing women's conferences, I jokingly tell the teenage girls that I want them so focused on their dreams that when some guy comes along and he's trying to get them to sleep with him, their attitude is, "That's sweet of you, but you see, getting pregnant at 16 is not on my vision board." But in all seriousness, I want our teenagers to be so focused on a dream God's put in their hearts that there's not a chance they would yield to drugs or premarital sex. I went online and googled a bunch of public school buildings, put them in my dream book and started asking God to let me teach teenagers to go after their dreams. "Whatever you ask in my name, this I will do, that the Father may be glorified in the Son" (John 14:13). Is the Father going to be glorified if I can impact teenagers? Absolutely. Now our vision board course and books are in schools across America teaching teenagers.

Start thinking of some big things you need to ask God for.

CHAPTER 2

Big

The Lord said, "Ask big and believe it's done." The second word that I want to talk with you about is *big*. Stop asking for things you think are possible.

If you can do it without God, it's not big enough.

Another statement Steve Harvey said is this, "Instead of praying for God to help you pay off your debts over the next seven years, think about the God we serve. He created the whole world in only six days, and it's going to take Him seven years to pay off your debt?" Think about that. I love what Myles Monroe said, "Whatever frightens you, that won't leave you, that's your dream." That's what you need to start asking God for.

If it's really that simple, why don't we start asking God?

Joyce Meyer says we pray "just" prayers. "Lord, if you'll *just* help me get through this. Lord, if you'll *just* help me survive this year. Lord, if you'll *just* help me get through this next semester." Do you know what *just* means? Barely enough to get by. Joyce said, "Stop trying to sound pitiful. You're not coming to God in your name. You're coming in the name of Jesus, and you're saying 'God I know I don't deserve this but I'm not coming in my name. I'm not coming in my power. I'm coming boldly in the name of Jesus.'" Joyce continued, "If God doesn't want you to have it, He won't give it to you anyway. But I would rather ask God for everything and get 50% then ask for nothing and get 100%."

Have you ever heard of the law of the rubber band? The law of the rubber band says if you want to go to the next level, you have to be stretched. Stretching is awkward. It's uncomfortable. It's painful sometimes. But it's necessary to go to the next level. Eric Thomas says, "If you want to go to the next level, you've got to get comfortable being uncomfortable."

So as you feel stretched, remember the law of the rubber band says that stretching is necessary.

Myles Monroe said God told him, "Ask me for something that makes me look like God."

Matthew 20 tells the story of when Jesus was walking down the road and He heard two blind men yelling, "Jesus, have mercy on us." What is interesting is how Jesus responded to them. He turned to the blind men and said, "What do you want me to do for you?" Doesn't that seem like a strange question? It seems like it's pretty obvious that they want their sight, right? Jesus asked them that question because He wanted to see what *they* were believing.

How they responded changed everything. They could have said, "Jesus, it's tough out here. You know we can't see, but could you *just* give us a place to live? Jesus, could you *just* help us get a job. Could you *just* give us some food?" He wanted to hear how big their faith was, because what they were asking was utterly impossible. They asked Him for their sight, and Jesus healed them.

I want you to imagine Jesus walking in to your house tonight and saying, "What do you want me to do for you?" How you respond is going to have a big impact on how your future unfolds. Imagine Him saying, "What do you want me to do?" And dare to ask Him for something big.

Joel Osteen had the audacity to ask God for the Compaq Center in Houston, TX to be his church. I want you to read this word-for-word because sometimes we look at people like the Osteens and think they just naturally have big faith. But listen to what Joel said, "Every voice in me was telling me, 'Who do you think you are? It's never going to happen. It's too big. You don't deserve it.'" But instead of believing those lies, he went to God and said, "God, I know it is far out, but I believe that you put this in our path for a reason so I'm asking you to make a way where I don't see a way." Reread that. "Make a way where I don't see a way." And not once did he feel God was saying, "Boy, you've got a lot of nerve asking me for something that big." In fact, he said the opposite, "I felt like God was pleased to see me asking for something that only He could do."

Pastor Michael Todd in Tulsa, Oklahoma had the audacity to ask God for the Spirit Bank Event Center to be his church. He admitted, "I wasn't even 100% sure it was God, and I felt like a fool asking for it." But today, his church owns that arena.

My dad, Jerry Savelle, at 74 years old had the audacity to ask God to give his ministry an international jet so he could fly overseas to minister. Some would ask, "Why does he need an expensive international jet at 74 years old?" But you know what? He had the audacity to ask God, and God had the audacity to give it to him. His ministry owns a Falcon 50 debt-free. I think Steve Harvey was right.

If you will up your ask,
God will up His give.

The Choke Hold

Each morning I take my Chocolate Labrador, Beauregard, on a walk. His leash is a reel that has a little button on it and if I push that button, the leash stops extending. Sometimes he will take off chasing rabbits and he is so big that I'm flying through the yard behind him pulling on his leash. But when I push that little button, it puts a choke hold on Beauregard. What does the choke hold do? It prevents him from going any further.

Every one of us have a choke hold that prevents us from going where we want to go. Where does God have to stop blessing you because you choke? Ladies, you might say, "I would easily spend $100 on a dress, but $500?" It's your choke hold. Or what about a house? "Yeah, I could envision living in a $700,000 house, but $2.7 million?" Choke. Or if you're in business, "I could imagine a $1 million revenue, but $20 million?" You choke. Where does God have to stop blessing you because you can't receive it? You choke and you won't even ask Him for something big.

Jesse Duplantis is the one who taught me this. Jesse and Cathy Duplantis' daughter Jodi is one of my dear friends, and years ago, they were visiting Jodi and her husband after they had just bought their brand new house. They were so proud. When Jesse and Cathy walked in, the house was pretty much empty.

Jodi explained where the furniture was going to be put. She told him, "Dad, I picked out this amazing rug, and the rug is going to go right here." She ran and got a picture of the rug to show him.

Jesse asked, "How much does that rug cost?"

Jodi said, "It's about $2,000. It's pretty expensive."

Jesse said he looked at Cathy, he gave her the eye, and he said, "Jodi, your mom and I want to get that rug for you. That's your house warming gift."

But Jodi said, "Dad! No, no, no. I did not show you that picture so that you would buy the rug for me. It's too much money. I can't let you do that."

Do you know what Jesse said? "Okay." And he walked off, got in the car, and went home.

Two months later, he went back to visit Jodi. He walked in the house, and it was pretty much still empty. He saw the windows had blinds on them, but they had no drapes. He said, "Jodi, when are you going to put some drapes on those windows?"

She said, "Dad, oh my goodness. I found this pattern. I found the fabric. I'm believing God for the money, but as soon as I get it all, I'm going to have these amazing drapes custom made."

Jesse said, "Well, how much does it cost?" She told him, and he said, "Go get the fabric.

Your mom and I are going to bless you. We're getting your drapes made."

"Dad, no!" She said, "You have no idea. It's not just one window. There are four windows. They're so expensive. I can't let you do that. It's too much."

What do you think Jesse said this time? "Okay." He got in his car, and he drove off.

Two years later, Jodi picked up her dad in her brand new car to take him to lunch. Jesse said, "Jodi, how much do you owe on this car."

She said, "I owe about $20,000."

He asked which bank she financed it through, and she told him. He said, "Let's drive to that bank right now. I'm going to pay your car off."

Jodi sat there a minute, and then she said, "Daddy, let the Lord lead you!" She took the choke hold off! They drove to that bank and within ten minutes she was driving a debt-free car. Jodi said, "Daddy, is that curtain and rug deal still on the table?"

The money was in the bank the whole time waiting for Jodi to take the choke hold off.

When are we really going to take God at His Word where He said, "Ask and you shall receive"? Take the choke hold off!

CHAPTER 3

Believe

The last part of what the Lord said is: "Believe it's done."

No matter what God has promised you, if your mind can't handle it, you won't receive it.

Jesse Duplantis tells the story from the early 70s when he was just starting to preach, driving an old beat up car from town-to-town, ministering in small churches. In fact, he used all the gas money he had, drove to one little church, preached his heart out, and all the pastor gave him for an offering was a can of Dr. Pepper. He went to a pay phone, called Cathy to tell her, and she said, "Well at least you're not thirsty Jesse."

Here's the thing, he was driving this little beat up car back home to New Orleans, when an airplane flew above him in the sky. When he looked up at that airplane, God dropped a dream in his heart, "One day, you're not going to be driving your little car to preach. You're going to be flying jets all over this world. You won't even be able to keep up with the engagements that you'll be going to." He sat there and thought, "But how could I pay for something like that?" And this statement absolutely changed Jesse Duplantis' entire life: God said, "Jesse I didn't ask you to pay for it. I asked you to believe for it."

Show God that You Believe

It's one thing to start asking God for the desires of your heart, but how do you show God that you truly believe He's capable of bringing them to pass? Here are five ways you show God that you believe:

#1 You envision it.

Habakkuk 2:2 says to write the vision, make it plain, so you can run towards it.

If you leave it in your head, it's not a vision, it's just your thoughts.

I want you to remember this phrase: If it's not on paper, it's a vapor. What is a vapor? A vapor is here today, gone tomorrow. It doesn't even exist anymore. So you cannot leave your dreams in your head. You have to take the time to write them down.

Years ago there was this motivational speaker and he met with a room full of Olympian hopefuls. He asked them, "How many of you have your dreams and goals in writing?" Every single hand went up. (That should tell us something, right?) Then he asked, "How many of you have your dreams and goals in writing with you right now?" One hand went up, and that one hand was Dan O'Brien who was the only person in the entire room who advanced and went on to win the gold medal. He said, "Never underestimate the power of having a dream and taking the time to write it down and keep it in front of you."

#2 You speak to it.

The Bible says that by faith the whole world was created (Hebrews 11:3). God created the entire world with the words of His mouth. Remember the story where Jesus was walking by a fig tree and He spoke to it and commanded it to wither up. (See Matthew 21:18-22 and Mark 11:12-25.)

But it didn't wither up instantly. The next day, the disciples were walking by, and when they saw the tree was withered up, they were shocked. Jesus looked at them like, "Come on. Have faith in God. Did you doubt for one minute?" But Jesus was trying to make a point to them. He thought of the smallest thing He could think of and said, "If you have faith the size of a mustard seed," and then He looked around for the biggest thing He could find, a mountain. He said, "If you have faith this small, you could speak to something that big, and it would have to obey you" (Author's paraphrase).

I want you to think about that. If you want to know where your life is headed, listen to the words that are coming out of your mouth.

> You've got to speak faith to your vision. Show God that you believe by speaking to that vision.

#3 You take action.

Faith without works or corresponding action is dead.

see James 2:17

Pastor Michael Todd said God told him to start buying TV equipment when he wasn't even on TV. God told my dad to go rent an airplane hangar when he didn't even have an airplane. When the paperwork asked the kind of airplane he had, he didn't even know what to tell them so he just wrote, "A nice one." He felt like a fool, but he was taking steps of faith and believed it was coming.

God told me to write my book before I had a publisher. God told me to print baby announcements before I was pregnant, because I was believing God that one day I was going to send those announcements out.

How does God want you to start taking action since faith without action is dead? Maybe you are believing to have your own ministry or business. Start getting the website ready. Maybe you are believing for a baby. Start picking out baby furniture. Has God called you to host conferences? Start calling hotels and find out what does it cost to rent a ballroom or arena or a coliseum.

Get the vision in front of you.

#4 You get your best seed in the ground.

The Bible says there are two things that will never pass away: The Word of God (Matthew 24:35) and seedtime and harvest (Genesis 8:22).

Every dream I've achieved in my life has required that I sow a seed, and certain times, my very best seed. I believe there will be times in your life when God asks you to give your best. Keep in mind that *your* best and someone else's best can be drastically different. I'll give you a couple examples.

When I was just a baby, my dad was going out of town to minister for several days and before leaving he gave my mom all the cash he had, which was only $3. That night my mom took me and my sister to church. Mom knew the money wasn't enough to meet the need over the coming days. Here's a key: When you are faced with your greatest need, sow your greatest seed. Prompted in her heart to give her best that night, she gave all $3 in the offering. After we returned home and she was changing, as she hung up her dress in the closet, she found $50 in one of the pockets! And that was enough to meet the need.

In 2007 I was on a trip to France and I fell in love with the precious people in this beautiful country. I had saved $500 and really wanted to buy something special because I didn't know if I'd ever go back. One day during this trip the Lord told me to give my best. I knew my best wasn't $200 of the $500. It was all of it. So instead of using it to buy something I really wanted, I gave it all to some pastors in Paris and trusted God was arranging things and how He wanted to use me. Six months after sowing that seed in France, I was ministering in Paris. By 2009, I had a book translated in French and was taking teams of ladies to minister there. In 2010, we had ICING Paris, and now we have seven ministry books translated in French.

That $500 seed (my best seed at the time) enabled God to open up a nation for me to minister in. What do you think? Was that a good decision to give that money rather than buy a souvenir or some t-shirts that said *J'aime Paris*? That decision changed my life and propelled me into my purpose.

Give God what you've got and He'll turn it into a lot! If you want supernatural growth, increase your giving. When God tells you to do something, it might take you by surprise or you might even say, "You've got to be kidding!" But if you give God what you've got, He'll turn what appears too small into something great when He gives you His all! You will be surprised to see what you can do with what He gives back to you.

Ephesians 3:20 Principle

Ephesians 3:20 says,

Now to him who is able to do exceedingly abundantly above all that we ask or think, according to the power that works in us.

I decided to wrap my faith around this verse and give according to it. If I want an Ephesians 3:20 harvest, I need to also sow an Ephesians 3:20 seed. I like having a "memorable offering" that ties in with what I'm believing. It's nothing magical; it's just a point of contact. I determined that we were going to sow "320" all year long. Whether it was $320 or $3,200 or $32,000, we were going to give and expect a year of abundant overflow of everything we're asking for!

So we started January off by giving our best Ephesians 3:20 offering, and we started asking big. Within three weeks we received the largest honorarium we've ever received in the history of the ministry, and we had more people enroll in our online teaching courses than the entire previous year! And that was all within three weeks!

Do you truly believe God can do "exceedingly, abundantly, above" in your life? Do you have faith for what you're asking even though you don't deserve it, you don't know how to do it, and it almost looks laughable? Do you have faith to present your requests in the name of Jesus and believe God will give you what you ask for?

Let me encourage you to sow for the harvest you want. Give your Ephesians 3:20

offering today. Whatever that means to you. It could be $32.00, $320, $3,200 or $32,000.

Here's what I've learned:

If your offering means something to you, it means something to God. Remember, we don't give because we have, we have because we give!

#5 You praise Him before it ever happens.

My dad, Jerry Savelle, says, "The depth of your praise determines the magnitude of your breakthrough." Have you ever watched *The Price is Right* when they'll announce, "You're the next contestant on *The Price is Right!*" These people are jumping and bouncing, going nuts. They haven't even won anything, but they sure act like they have. That's the way you need to act when you go to God every day presenting your requests. Thank Him before you ever see the breakthrough. Start praising Him as if it's already happened.

Praise is the highest expression of faith. I like to do it so much that it freaks the devil out. I've done this many times when we're in Paris. I'll turn to my friends and say, "I have an apartment in Paris, France! Thank you, Jesus!" My friends will say, "You do? When did you get the apartment?" And I'll say, "Well, in Jesus' name!" But I like to do it so convincingly that not only does it get the attention of God but it also confuses the devil out so much that he's thinking, "Did I miss something?" That's part of tormenting the devil.

So praise God before the breakthrough.

Action Step

On the following page I have a form I want you to fill out. I want you to be thinking and praying about the three biggest things you're going to ask God for and apply God's Word to them. Fill out those three big things on this form.

But I also want to pray over these with you. I believe there is power in prayer. Where two or more agree on something there's power. Simply go to www.terri.com/askbig and send me your three biggest asks. My team and I are going to pray over them and believe God that there's an acceleration taking place. Things that should normally take five years are going to manifest with supernatural speed!

Write down your three biggest requests (asks). What are you believing God for that looks utterly impossible right now? It's not a vision if it only remains in your thoughts. Get it on paper.

Next, give an Ephesians 3:20 offering. What does that mean? Give something that stretches you, that's memorable, that causes you to put a demand on your faith for those dreams.

Finally, declare Ephesians 3:20 every day. Memorize it. Print it out. Put it on your phone screen saver and act as if your three biggest requests are truly done in Jesus' name!

I'm cheering you on!

"Ask big and believe it's done"

The three biggest things I'm believing for:

---

1. ______________________________

2. ______________________________

3. ______________________________

"Now to him who is able to do exceedingly abundantly above all that we ask or think, according to the power that works in us."

Ephesians 3:20

Terri Savelle Foy is a world-class motivator who teaches that if you can dream it, God can do it. Through personal experience and proven results, she is helping people discover how to develop vision, confidence and discipline that will lead them into God's perfect plan for their lives. Terri's television show, Live Your Dreams, and weekly podcast have become a source of inspiration and a lifeline of hope for many around the globe.

OTHER BOOKS BY TERRI SAVELLE FOY

Make Your Dreams Bigger Than Your Memories

Imagine Big

Untangle

The Leader's Checklist

Pep Talk

Dream it. Pin it. Live it.

Declutter Your Way to Success

5 Things Successful People Do Before 8 AM